WINDSOR CREEK ELEMENTARY
Windsor Unified School District
9291 Old Redwood Hwy. Bldg. 300, Ste. C
Windsor, California 95492

– Fast Tracks

–Vintage Car Racing

A.T. McKenna

visit us at
www.abdopub.com

Published by Abdo & Daughters, 4940 Viking Drive, Suite 622, Edina, Minnesota 55435.
Copyright © 1998 by Abdo Consulting Group, Inc., Pentagon Tower, P.O. Box 36036, Minneapolis, Minnesota 55435 USA. International copyrights reserved in all countries. No part of this book may be reproduced in any form without written permission from the publisher.

Printed in the United States.

Cover and Interior Photo credits: Allsport USA, Super Stock

Edited by Paul Joseph

Library of Congress Cataloging-in-Publication Data

McKenna, A. T.
    Vintage car racing / A. T. McKenna.
       p.   cm. -- (Fast tracks)
  Includes index.
  Summary: Describes the four classes of vintage cars, how they are restored and rebuilt, and the unique aspects of classic car races.
    ISBN 1-56239-834-2
  1. Automobile racing--Juvenile literature. 2. Antique and classic cars--Juvenile literature. [1. Automobile racing.] I. Title. II. Series: McKenna, A.T. Fast tracks.
  GV1029.M46 1998
  796.72--dc21
                                       97-38920
                                        CIP
                                        AC

−Contents

–Vintage Car Racing

Vintage car racing is a new form of racing to most parts of the United States. England and other European countries have been enjoying vintage auto racing for years. Racers fix up old race cars and run them in competition. All types of people race vintage race cars. Drivers are both young and old. There are as many women as men competing in this unique form of auto racing.

Vintage auto racing is different from other types of racing because the emphasis is on fun, not on competition. In the United States, there isn't a championship series in which drivers receive points like other types of auto racing. There usually isn't a cash award for winning the race. Aggressive, fast racing is not acceptable in vintage auto racing. Drivers take great care in preparing the cars which are very rare and irreplaceable.

Vintage race cars come in a variety of shapes and sizes. Many vintage race cars are convertibles. Some of the cars are very old and rare. Other cars are newer, usually from the 1960s and earlier.

Vintage race cars come from all classes of auto racing. They can be sports cars, such as Ferraris and Maseratis. They can also be old Formula 1 cars, drag racers, sprint cars, or midget racers. Vintage race cars can also be G.T. or Grand Touring cars such as

Jaguars, Lotus', Fiat-Abarths, MGs, and Triumphs. Since these cars are all very different, there are different organizations and regulations for each type. Usually, a vintage drag racer does not race against a Porsche. Similar types of cars race in the same class. Classes can be broken down by years and type of car.

Vintage racing includes cars from all classes of auto racing.

–Classes of Cars

Although there are many different types of vintage racing cars, there are four main classes that most of the cars fit into. The first group is Pre-World War II. These cars were made much more simple than modern cars. The driver sometimes had to pump the oil into the engine with a hand pump. Yet the cars were able to reach speeds of 90 miles per hour (145 kph). Some of the cars in this class include Bugatti, Maserati, BMW, Jaguar SS, Ford Model T, Bentley, and Studebaker.

The next group of cars are Vintage and Historic Production Sports Cars. These are production sports cars like Austin-Healey, MG, Alfa Romeo, Corvette, Lotus, and Porsche. A production car means that the car is just like the ones you see on the streets, with some added parts. The cars must have been produced between 1960 and 1968 to be in this class. These cars are very close in performance, racing at speeds above 140 miles per hour (225 kph).

The third class is Vintage and Historic Sports Racing Cars. These cars were made specifically for racing. These cars have to have certain parts, including two seats, wheels covered by fenders, doors, lights, and a horn. Some of the cars include Ferrari, Porsche, Lola, Lotus, and Can-Am racers.

The last class is Formula cars. These include Formula Junior class cars from 1957-1959. The class also includes Formula 1 and Formula 2 cars from 1960-1963. Some famous racers who drove these cars are Juan Manuel Fangio, Jim Clark, and Graham Hill. The Vintage Sports Car Club of America (VSCCA) is one of many vintage automobile racing sanctioning bodies. A sanctioning body is an organization which makes the rules and regulations for the group of auto racers. The Vintage Sports Car Club of America is the very first vintage auto racing organization.

It began in 1958. Other sanctioning bodies set their rules based on the rules of the VSCCA. This group is very strict. Only cars from 1959 and earlier are allowed to compete in Vintage Sports Car Club of America races. The VSCCA's motto is to have fun with old cars. Because of this, they don't keep track of winners or lap times.

This 1963 Lotus 63 is a perfect example of a vintage racer.

—Restoring the Car

Since vintage race cars are cars that have already been built, putting the car together isn't the same as with other types of race cars. Vintage race car drivers must restore and rebuild the car. Unless you are skilled at automotive repair, it is best to take the car to a professional body shop that specializes in vintage automobile repair.

The first component on a vintage race car is the chassis or roll cage. The chassis looks like the skeleton of a car. The chassis consists of several pieces of metal welded together to form a frame for the car. All sharp edges on the chassis must be smoothed before putting them together. All pieces must fit perfectly in order for the chassis to work. The chassis must be very strong to protect the driver if there is a crash.

The chassis is one of the most important parts of a vintage automobile. This is the part that will corrode or show wear the most. In order to restore the chassis, the body and other pieces of the car must be removed to get to the chassis.

One of the best ways to learn how to restore a chassis on a particular vintage race car is to find others who have the same car. There are vintage car clubs for all types of cars. These clubs are

A vintage car must be in top shape to be allowed to race.

very helpful in giving information about the cars and where to find parts for these old cars.

The first step in preparing the chassis is to clean it. Every corner, seam, and edge of the car needs to be scrubbed clean so that damage can be found. Rust is one of the biggest problems with vintage cars. If you don't completely clean the chassis, sometimes rust can go unnoticed. If the car has rust, it must be removed before continuing to restore the rest of the car.

In vintage auto racing, a racer is not allowed to compete without restoring the body of the car. The body is placed on top of the chassis and is the outside part of the car that everyone sees. It is painted and a racing number is placed on both sides of the car, usually on the doors. The body is usually made of some type of metal.

On vintage cars, most of the body was made by hand by the original car builder. It was made to fit the chassis perfectly when the car was first made. But as the race car gets older, the body can sometimes stretch and may not fit the chassis as well. Sometimes you can tell the body has stretched when you hear or feel rattling noises when driving the car. If the body has stretched, it means air is getting through, which could make the car go slower on the track.

Although vintage auto racers are not allowed to add new pieces to the body to stop air from flowing in, there are some techniques you can use. Some parts can be covered, such as the passenger side of the cockpit to stop air flow. You can also tape up parts that are hanging under the body and remove pieces such as the radio antenna and windshield wipers. When the body is properly restored, you shouldn't see any big gaps or spaces.

Vintage racers are not allowed to add extra pieces to a car.

–Just Like New

Once the body of the car is assembled, the car is given a fresh coat of paint. The car should have a light coat of new paint in the original color. Applying too many layers of paint can affect the car's performance. The driver's name is sometimes painted on the door or near the windshield on a vintage racer.

Rules specify where the car number should be displayed on the car and the minimum size the number must be. The car number is painted on both sides of the car and on the roof of the car so it can be seen from all angles. Some cars must also have the number on the back or trunk of the car. The car now looks almost like new.

After the chassis and body are restored, the engine and parts must be repaired. The engine size on a vintage racer will depend on the type of car. Most organizations require that the original engine be used. Many times this means that the engine will have to be rebuilt by an engine builder if the racer does not have the skills. Repairing the engine is often the most expensive part of vintage racing.

Racing a car can cause strain to the engine due to the added heat and vibrations racing causes. If a vintage race car was raced for several years when it was new, it means that the engine was strained quite a bit.

The first step is to clean the engine and the compartment where the engine is placed. This is important for inspection before the race. It also helps prevent fires in the engine caused by grease and oil spots.

All the hoses in the engine for the oil and fuel should be replaced with new stainless steel hoses. Every rubber belt should be replaced with a new belt. All the wires in the engine should be wrapped with fire resistant tape or tied together to prevent rubbing on parts of the engine and causing a fire.

Once repairs are made, it is time to check for leaks of the oil, fuel, or water. If the car leaks oil or fuel onto the race track, the driver could be disqualified from the race. The driver should let the car run for a short while and then check the ground for any spills.

Rebuilding the engine is the most expensive part of vintage racing.

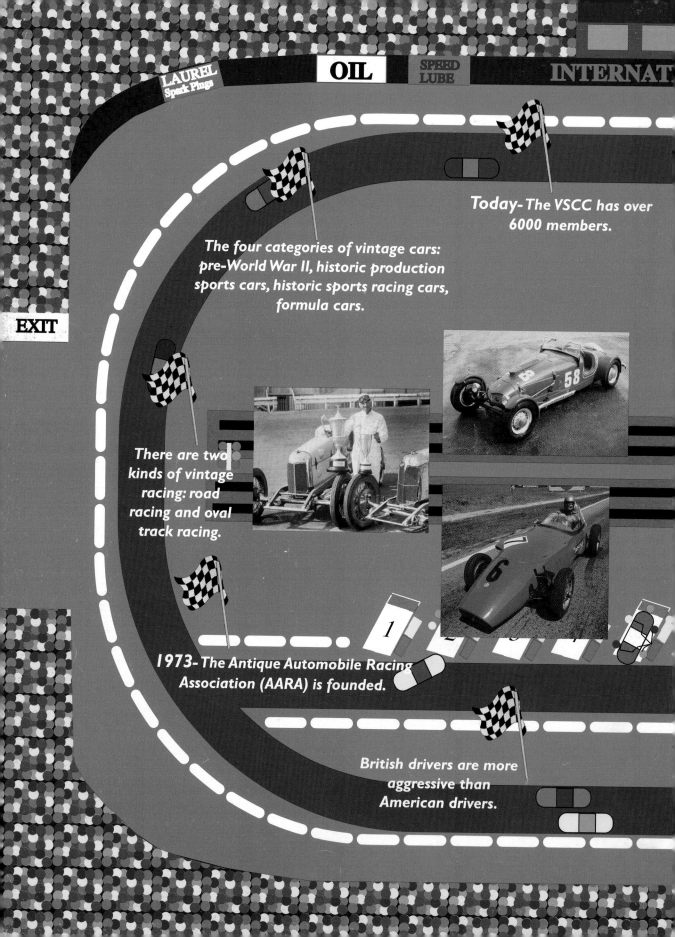

LAUREL
Spark Plugs

OIL

SPEED
LUBE

INTERNAT

EXIT

Today- The VSCC has over 6000 members.

The four categories of vintage cars: pre-World War II, historic production sports cars, historic sports racing cars, formula cars.

There are two kinds of vintage racing: road racing and oval track racing.

1973- The Antique Automobile Racing Association (AARA) is founded.

British drivers are more aggressive than American drivers.

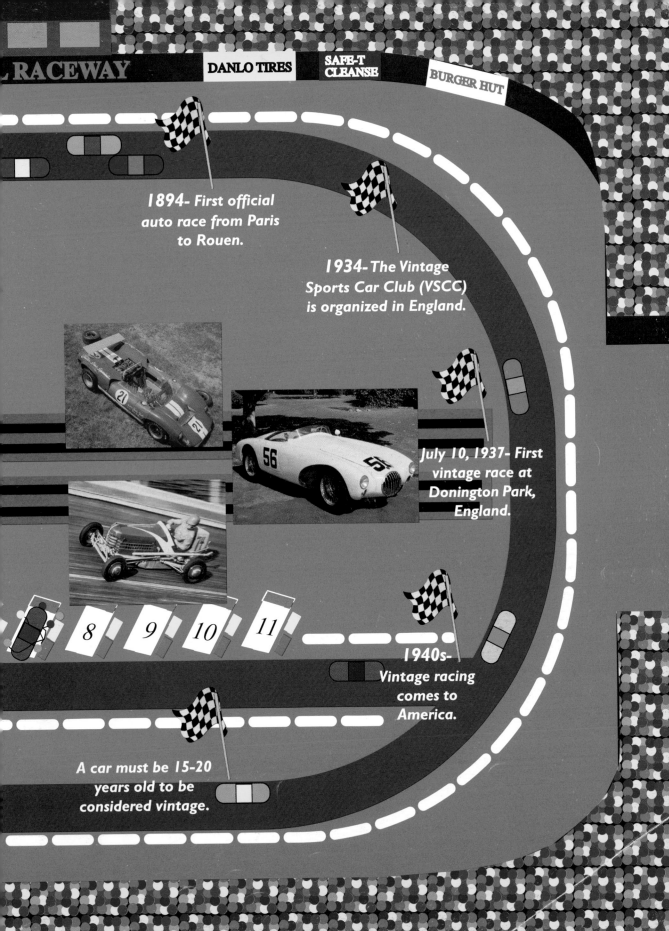

1894- First official auto race from Paris to Rouen.

1934- The Vintage Sports Car Club (VSCC) is organized in England.

July 10, 1937- First vintage race at Donington Park, England.

1940s- Vintage racing comes to America.

A car must be 15-20 years old to be considered vintage.

8 9 10 11

—*Wheels & Tires*

Just like the cars, vintage racing tires and wheels come in a variety of styles and sizes, depending on the type of car. There are wire wheels, alloy wheels, and wooden wheels. Checking and replacing the wheels is particularly important in vintage auto racing, since old wheels can break down while racing. Wire wheels have spokes that can loosen or break. Alloy wheels can bend or crack. And wood spokes can do everything from loosen, break, bend, and even rot! Keep the wheels clean and check them often for damage.

The tires that were originally on your vintage race car will need to be replaced. Old tires are usually hard and cracked due to the materials they used to be made from. Most vintage auto racing organizations require molded treaded tires. The tread is the grooved face of a tire. It's the part of the tire that touches the ground. The tread depth, or deepness of the grooves, must be at least 1/32 inch.

The width and diameter of the tires depends on the rules of the organization. Usually the maximum width of the tire allowed is what will fit inside the wheel wells (the curved spot on the body of the car where the wheels go) without changing the body of the car. Tires for vintage racers are hard to find and can cost a lot. Dunlop makes a few tires in the old vintage patterns, but there aren't many sizes available. Many racers have to use street tires which are for everyday cars. They shave down the rubber and put grooves in just to be able to race.

Finding tires for this 1942 Stanguellini can be difficult.

−Breaking Fast

The safety of the driver depends on the brakes. If there is another race car or debris in the way, the driver has to be confident that the car will stop. The driver also needs to use the brakes when going around a turn. And since vintage race cars are often rare, and repairs expensive, brakes are very important.

Inside the car, the brake pedal is placed very close to the accelerator (gas pedal) so the driver can use the heel of the foot to brake, and the toes to increase speed. While racing, there is no time to take the foot completely off the brake and then put it on the gas pedal. The driver must do both at the same time. This is the "heel/toe" system.

Vintage race car brakes are much stronger than regular brakes. The brakes must be made to hold up to the heat created when a driver must brake fast. Most vintage racers prefer that the brake pedal is harder, so the car stops more quickly and won't slide very far.

Racing brake pads must also be very strong. The old brake pads should be replaced with new pads made of a carbon/metal mix which helps stand up to the heat and prevents the pads from wearing out too quickly. Sometimes one set of brake pads only lasts one race.

–Filling Fuel

Most vintage race cars use gasoline. The type of gasoline must be 100 octane in order to make the engine run properly. Octane is a substance in the gasoline that is made of carbon and hydrogen.

High octane gas (100 octane or over) is used in race cars and in aircraft. The problem is, most regular gas stations don't carry 100 octane gas. A vintage racer can make the octane higher by adding

A 1930 Ford V-8 "Special".

octane boosters, which are made by companies such as Moroso and Vortex. Adding a quart of the booster to 20 gallons of gas will make the octane 100 or more. Great care must be taken in mixing the gas, since the chemicals are toxic. Some small airports may sell the 100 octane gas to racers and some tracks may have racing gas available on race day.

–Suiting Up Safely

Different vintage racing organizations have different rules on the cars. But when it comes to driver gear, every piece of clothing the driver wears must be made of special safety materials. Drivers must wear driving suits which are fireproof and usually made of a material called Nomex. Socks, gloves, shoes, even underwear must also be fireproof. This is to protect the driver in case of an engine fire while driving or during a crash.

A high-quality helmet is one of the most important pieces of the driver's gear. The helmet could save a driver's life during a crash, especially since many vintage cars are convertibles. There are vents in the helmet to keep the driver cool. Most helmets are painted in the driver's favorite colors, or painted to match the car colors.

While helmets and fire resistant suits are very important items, there are a few other things a driver must have before jumping in the car. All drivers should carry a fire extinguisher in the car while racing. Most vintage racing organizations require this. Many tracks also require a safety harness, which is just like a seat belt. Drivers should never chew gum or have anything in their mouth such as candy that could get caught in their throat while racing. Drivers should not take any medicine if they are racing. It could affect reaction time and reflexes. Drivers should paint their name, age, and any medical information on their helmet. Drivers should not wear contact lenses, but shatterproof glasses instead. All loose items should be taken out of the cockpit, the driving suit, and the trunk of the car.

Drivers in the 1948 Indianapolis 500 did not have the high-tech gear that todays drivers have.

–How to Start Racing

One of the best ways to get involved in vintage auto racing is to go to the races. Local racing tracks have information on the different series and when the events are held.

There are more than 40 vintage racing clubs in the United States alone to find out about races. Some events are by invitation only with strict rules and regulations regarding the race cars. Others are open to anyone with an interest and who has the required safety equipment.

Going to a professional driving school is a great way to try out the sport of vintage racing. Schools will supply the cars, helmets, and driving suits to someone interested in trying vintage racing for a fee. Most tracks require that a driver is at least 18 years old and has a valid driver's license.

Another good way to get involved in vintage auto racing is to volunteer at the track. There is a need for registration people, tech inspectors, corner workers, and safety crews. Some of these workers plan to own and race a vintage car someday and they are gaining valuable knowledge.

–At the Track

Many vintage car races take place on tracks that are oval. An oval track is shaped like an egg. The cars race around the tracks in one direction, counter-clockwise. Most of the crashes and bumping into the walls happens on the curves. The long length of the track is called the straight-away. This is the area where the driver can really pick up speed. The start/finish line is located in the middle of the straight-away.

There are also many vintage auto races that take place on road courses. These courses vary in distance from race to race. Road race courses zig zag around the city or countryside. Many road races are held on regular streets which are blocked off for the race. Road courses can run from town to town, or even country to country.

Many vintage race tracks allow testing of the cars to make sure the car is running properly. Testing is particularly helpful for a new racer or a driver who will be racing a different car. It's a chance to check how the engine is performing and if the brakes are working or not. Drivers can compare lap times and figure out how the car is handling at high speeds.

Testing times and rules vary from track to track. Most testing takes place a few weeks before a race. For safety reasons, tracks require that racers have a vehicle for transporting the car or the driver in case of an emergency. A driver must have a friend to help keep track of lap times and check the pressure of the tires. The driver must have safety equipment such as a fireproof suit, helmet, and fire extinguisher on hand. A small fee is charged for testing.

As with other forms of auto racing, vintage cars must also pass a pre-race inspection.

-Race Day

Before a vintage car driver can compete on the race track, the car must pass a technical inspection. Inspections take place right before the race begins. Inspectors are looking for items that will affect the safety of the driver. They look for oil, water, and gas leaks, problems with wheels and tires, and make sure the parts on the cars are the original ones. Rules are very strict. If an item on the car is the wrong size, or not an original piece, the car can be disqualified from the race. Officials also open the hood of the car and check the engine and the other parts inside. The engine and engine compartment must be clean. The car must be painted and the numbers properly displayed. No rusty or unrestored cars are allowed to compete. Once a car passes inspection, a safety sticker is placed on the car that allows the car on the track.

On race day, the driver arrives early to get registered for the race. Last minute repairs are made off the track and all the parts of the car are checked and re-checked to make sure the car is ready to race. A driver may do the repairs or may have a friend or family member help out. Sometimes vintage auto racers help each other out. It's a friendly atmosphere at the race track.

The car is then pushed out to the starting grid, the area on the track where the race will start. Marks on the starting grid show where the cars are to be placed. Veteran racers (those who have raced before) are usually placed in the front rows. Rookies (new racers) are placed in following rows. The cars must stay in their places until the green flag waves and the start/finish line is crossed.

During the race, vintage racers are expected to show respect

*The Daytona Fire Cracker 400
Race in the 1960's.*

for both the car they are driving, as well as other cars on the track. If a driver starts racing dangerously, he or she is asked to leave. Racers who dent or damage their own cars or someone else's are not allowed to race for the rest of the year.

A car may pull over to get more fuel, but during the race, no repairs are made. Tires are not changed and parts are not replaced. If the car breaks down, it is out of the race. That is why preparing the car properly before the race is so important.

−Waving the Flags

Racers need to know when to start the race, when to pull over to the side of the track, and when to stop. A track official waves many different colored flags during the race to tell the racer what to do.

A green flag is used to signal the start of the race. When a driver sees the green flag waving, it means "GO." A yellow flag tells the drivers to be careful, stop passing, and there might be a dangerous situation ahead. A red flag means the race is being stopped.

Drivers are usually instructed to go into the side of the track or line up in a certain area when there is a red flag waving. A black flag pointed at a certain driver's car means the driver must leave the track immediately. This flag means the car may not be safe to drive, or the driver is racing dangerously. A white flag means that the leader of the race has started the last lap of the race. Only one lap to go! The black and white checkered flag is the flag waved when the winning car crosses the finish line.

<u>*−Winning Isn't*</u>
<u>*−Everything*</u>

Vintage racing is not like other types of racing where the winner receives money and big prizes. The sport of vintage auto racing has more to do with having fun and enjoying, restoring, and racing an old car. Most vintage racers pick the type of car they race because they find them interesting, not because the car is the fastest.

Many vintage auto racing organizations don't keep track of scores or lap times. Most don't even record official winners. For racers and spectators alike, it's a chance to see and hear old race cars that would otherwise be in a museum on display, or in someone's garage. Vintage auto racing isn't about winning, it's about having fun!

Opposite page: Vintage racing competition is not as fierce as it was in 1931 when this picture was taken.

–Glossary

Accelerator - Gas pedal on the floor of the driver's side.

Alloy wheels - Wheels that are made from a mixture of different metals.

Body - The part of the car which fits over the chassis. It is the outside part of the car that everyone sees. The body is hand-crafted most of the time.

Chassis - The frame of the car. The chassis is like the skeleton of the car.

Convertible - Cars which don't have a roof or top on them.

Corrode - To wear away or dissolve.

Flags - Different colored flags that help direct the drivers on the race track. Some flags mean stop, some mean go, and some are warning flags.

Fire Extinguisher - A container which is filled with chemicals to help put out a fire.

G.T. - "Grand Touring" cars such as Jaguars, Lotus', Fiat-Abarths, MGs, and Triumphs.

Inspection - All cars must pass requirements for the height, weight, and equipment used in and on the car. Cars are inspected before the race.

Nomex - A fireproof material used for driving suits and other driver clothing.

Octane - A substance in the gasoline that is made of carbon and hydrogen.

Ovals - Tracks which are shaped like an egg. The cars race around the tracks in one direction, counter-clockwise.

Production Car - The car is just like the ones you see on the streets, with some added parts.

Road Courses - Tracks that zig zag around the city or countryside. Some road races go from town to town or country to country.

Safety harness - The special seat belt which keeps the driver from moving around while racing.

Safety Sticker - The racer receives a safety sticker when the car passes inspection and is safe to be on the track. This sticker goes on the car.

Sanctioning Body - The organization that sets the rules for racing.

Spectators - People who come to watch the race.

Starting grid - The area on the track where the cars line up to begin the race.

Testing - Vintage racers sometimes pay a fee to drive around the track and test their car before competing in a race.

Tire pressure - The amount of air that is put in the tire.

Track Official - Someone who works for the track and makes sure the rules are being followed. A track official waves the different flags to let the drivers know what to do.

Tread - The grooved face of a tire. It's the part of the tire that touches the ground.

Vintage Sports Car Club of America (VSCCA) - One of many vintage automobile racing sanctioning bodies.

Wheel Wells - The curved spot on the body of the car where the wheels fit.

—*Internet Sites*

Formula 1 Links Heaven
http://ireland.iol.ie/~roym/
This site includes official sites, latest news, drivers, teams, computer games, circuits, mailing lists. This site has sound and video, very colorful and interactive.

Drag Racing on the net
http://www.lm.com/~hemi/
This is a cool and interactive sight with sound and fun photos.

Indyphoto.com
http://www.indyphoto.com/index.htm
This award winning site has excellent photographs of Indy Cars and it is updated on a regular basis.

MotorSports Image Online
http://www.msimage.com/index2.htm
This site gives you standings, results, schedules, teams, news, and a photo gallery.

Extreme Off-Road Racing
http://www.calpoly.edu/~jcallan/
This site has pre-runners, chat rooms, videos, racing pictures, wrecks, links, and much more extreme off-road racing stuff.

These sites are subject to change. Go to your favorite search engine and type in car racing for more sites.

Pass It On

Racing Enthusiasts: educate readers around the country by passing on information you've learned about car racing. Share your little-known facts and interesting stories. Tell others what your favorite kind of car is or who your favorite racer is. We want to hear from you!

To get posted on the ABDO & Daughters website E-mail us at "Sports@abdopub.com"

Visit the ABDO & Daughter website at www.abdopub.com

−*Index*